Am

Milner Craft Series

EMBROIDERED

INITIALS

Christine Harris

First published in 1991 by
Sally Milner Publishing Pty Ltd
at 'The Pines'
RMB 54 Burra Road
Burra Creek NSW 2620
Australia

© Christine Harris, 1995
Reprint 1997

Design and layout by Olev Muska

Photography by Andrew Elton

Film by Sphere Color Graphics Pty. Limited, Brisbane

Printed in Australia by Impact Printing, Melbourne

National Library of Australia

Cataloguing-in-Publication data:

Harris, Christine, 1947-.
 Embroidered initials.

 ISBN 1 86351 177 6.

 1. Embroidery. 2. Needlework. I. Title. (Series: Milner craft series).

746.44

CONTENTS

ACKNOWLEDGEMENTS

I would like to thank Diana de Hautecloque of Stadia Handcrafts, Paddington for supplying the beads, buttons and charms used in this book.

I would also like to thank Sally Milner and her staff for their invaluable assistance, in particular Liz Kaydos and Lisa Hanrahan.

Thank you to my friend Virginia Bowden for the use of her computer and for the time she has given so willingly, and to my daughter Susan for her help.

*A*lphabets have long been popular with embroiderers. Possibly as far back as the seventeenth century, alphabets have been incorporated into samplers, although only twenty-four letters were used originally. Young girls began to embroider at an early age, starting with a simple alphabet. In Victorian times, monograms were very popular. Girls would stitch them on their personal clothing and on linen, sheets, handkerchiefs, towels and other household goods for their trousseau. Cross-stitch alphabets have also been popular for most of this century and there are some delightful designs available today.

In this book I hope to provide today's embroiderers with some ideas that are an extension of the simple alphabets that we have seen in the past, providing the designs for more elaborate and creative lettering which will have a multitude of uses. A single initial framed would make a special gift. Perhaps add a charm that is appropriate for the occasion – for example, a key for a twenty-first gift, or something that reflects

reflects the interests of the person who is to receive the gift. Initials of the bride and groom would make a lovely ring cushion. Whatever project you choose, I hope that you enjoy working your embroidered initials.

The photographs in this book show the embroidery enlarged to approximately 120% while the drawings show the actual size in which Christine has worked them.

THINGS YOU SHOULD KNOW BEFORE YOU START

☛ Use an embroidery hoop for all but the bullion stitches.

☛ Always use a very sharp pencil to transfer the design onto your fabric. If you use a blunt pencil, you will end up with a thick line that may not be covered well by your embroidery. A thicker line may also smudge as you are working and soil the fabric.

☛ Do not be concerned if you cannot fit in every detail exactly as shown on the stitch key. Everyone works at a slightly different tension, so the number of flowers worked by each stitcher may vary.

☛ If you prefer not to incorporate any of the charms, buttons or beads, you can either omit the beads completely or substitute them with french knots. You can replace the charms and buttons with flowers.

☛ The colours used are intended as a guide only. You may substitute them with colours of your choice. If you intend working more than one letter – that is, a name or set of initials – I suggest that if you use different colours for each letter, you use the same green throughout.

☛ When incorporating buttons or charms into your design, stitch the button/charm in position before you begin the embroidery. If using a double-sided charm, split the charm and use one side only. The charm will have a ring at the top; stitch around this ring with a satin stitch and finish with a french knot in the centre so that it looks like a flower. If possible, catch the charm in one or two inconspicuous places with a single thread so that the charm sits flat on your fabric.

☛ If using a plastic button with a shank similar to the cameo button used in the letter 'I', you must first remove the shank. Secure the flat bottom to the fabric with a little craft glue.

☛ You may simplify or modify the designs to suit other thread types. A simplified version of one of the letters surrounded by a garland of flowers worked in wool would make a wonderful gift for a baby or a knee rug for an older person.

☛ You can increase the size of the initials by enlarging the designs on a photocopier. You will need to remember to increase the number of threads you use and also to use a larger needle to increase the size of the flowers.

☞ The designs are drawn with the flowers shown actual size. Try to keep to this scale. The coloured photographs have been enlarged slightly. They are not shown actual size.

☞ All daisies and forget-me-nots have a lemon (No. 745) french knot centre.

☞ All french knots have one twist unless otherwise stated.

CHOOSING AN ALPHABET

$\mathcal{T}$here are many lovely alphabets available today and these can be obtained from a variety of sources. Embroidery, art or calligraphy books all provide ideas. The size of the letter you choose does not matter, as it can be enlarged or reduced using a photocopier. It is necessary only to have a basic outline to work with, and then you can enjoy designing your own embroidered initial. Trace the basic outline onto paper as described on pages 7-8, then draw in the flowers that you intend to use. Begin at the centre of the line or curve by placing the largest flower or cluster of flowers at or near the centre. As you work towards the outer edges of this line or curve, decrease the size and number of flowers used.

The embroidered letters could be quite small, in which case you would probably use only a single strand of thread. Letters could be as small as 1cm (½"); a letter of this size might be worked entirely in french knots to form tiny flowers. Large letters up to 15-20cm (6-8") could be worked in much the same way as the initials contained in this book; the given design can be worked with up to six strands of thread for the larger flowers and the number of threads reduced accordingly for the smaller flowers, leaves and stems.

Transferring the Design

*U*sing any relatively transparent paper – for example, tracing paper, tissue paper or greaseproof paper – place it over your chosen design, then with a soft lead pencil, draw a line through the centre of the design. Use this line as the basis for drawing up your embroidery design.

Transfer the design onto your fabric with the aid of a light box. If a light box is not available, you can improvise by using a window so that the sun acts as the light source, or by placing a lamp under a glass coffee table.

Tape the design to the glass, and place the fabric over the design, making sure that the design is centred. Using a very sharp soft lead pencil, trace the design onto the fabric so that you have a very fine, light line. It is not necessary to mark in every flower, just a dot for the largest flowers or clusters of flowers will do. Then follow the stitch key to complete the design.

OTHER INFORMATION

THREADS

The colours suggested throughout the designs are for DMC stranded cottons. There are many beautiful threads available today. Some of the hand-dyed cottons would be ideal for this type of work. Stranded silks would also be lovely on a silk background, but bear in mind that most of these silks are a little heavier than the stranded cottons; you will either need to increase the size of the design slightly or simplify it so that less flowers are required. Be prepared to experiment a little to find threads that appeal to you and give you the result that you are looking for.

LAUNDRY

Any embroidery that is to be framed should always be laundered. Carefully hand wash the completed project in a mild laundry detergent. Rinse very thoroughly and dry in the shade.

Gently press with the embroidery right side down into a folded towel.

Care should be taken to check the manufacturer's instructions regarding washing instructions before purchasing any fabrics.

FABRICS

Many fabrics are suitable for this type of embroidery; damask, silk, taffeta or linen are but a few suggestions. In choosing a fabric, it is important to select one that is closely woven, as the embroidery is very fine and the french knots may easily disappear through to the back of a more open-weave fabric.

MARKING PENS

I tend not to use any of the water soluble or fade away pens or transfer pencils as they can be difficult to remove. All that is required is a soft lead pencil (2B) or a very fine lead pencil such as a Pacer. Lead pencil washes out easily and leaves no unwanted residue.

NEEDLES

I have used a No. 10 crewel needle for all the embroidery.

Many embroiderers, however, find this size needle too fine and therefore difficult to thread. If this is the case for you, you may find a No. 9 more suitable. If you chose to embellish any of the embroidery with Mill Hill Petite beads, though, you may have to persevere and use the finer needle, or a beading needle if you have one; as the name of the beads implies, they are very small and therefore have a small hole through the centre.

STITCH GLOSSARY

AISIES

DAISY ~ Five lazy-daisy petals with a french knot centre.

DAISY BUD ~ Two or three lazy-daisy petals with a french knot centre.

LARGE DAISY ~ Seven or eight lazy-daisy petals with two or three french knots in the centre.

LONG-TACK DAISY ~ Three long-tack lazy-daisy petals.

BULLION DAISY ~ Five straight bullion stitches of eight wraps each. Work a lazy-daisy stitch around each bullion so that this stitch surrounds the bullion.

ROSES

ROSE ~ The number of bullion stitches that form the centre of the rose are indicated on the stitch key. Work the centre first, which consists of two or three straight bullions of eight wraps each, side by side. Then work five or six curved bullion stitches of twelve wraps each around the central bullions.

ROSEBUD ~ Work in the same way as the rose, that is, two or three straight centre bullions with three curved bullion stitches at one end.

SMALL ROSEBUD ~ Two straight bullion stitches of eight wraps each, side by side.
NOTE: All of the small rosebuds are surrounded by a single fly stitch.

STRAIGHT STITCH FLOWERS

SMALL STARS ~ Five small straight stitch petals of about 1mm (¹⁄₁₆") in length with a french knot centre.

SATIN STITCH FLOWERS ~ Five small straight stitch petals. Each petal has two straight stitches, one worked exactly on top of the other, beginning and ending in exactly the same hole.

ASTER ~ Six to ten straight stitches worked in a circle.

BUD ~ Three straight stitches.

STRAIGHT STITCH ~ Short straight stitches, often worked along a tendril to form a spray.

FUCHSIA ~ A french knot with three small straight stitches to one side.

BUTTONHOLE FLOWERS

BUTTONHOLE FLOWER ~ Work a circle of buttonhole stitch. Some of the buttonhole flowers have a french knot centre.

BUTTONHOLE BUD ~ A small section of the buttonhole circle.

STEMS, LEAVES, TENDRILS AND OTHER GREENERY

STEMS AND TENDRILS ~ All of the stems and tendrils are couched in position.

LEAVES ~ All leaves are a simple lazy-daisy stitch, either single or worked in clusters.

FLY STITCH ~ A fly stitch surrounds each small rosebud. The tacking or couching stitch at the end of the fly stitch may be long or short, depending on what will fit in.

STRAIGHT STITCH GREENERY ~ Small straight stitches worked along or at the end of stems or tendrils.

FRENCH KNOT GREENERY ~ Single twist, single strand french knots.

LAVENDER ~ A series of straight bullion stitches of about twelve wraps each. Work the central bullion with six or eight bullion stitches closely together, alternating down to form the spray.

 FORGET-ME-NOT ~ All forget-me-nots have a central lemon (No. 745) knot with five evenly spaced, single twist french knots surrounding the centre.

 CHAIN STITCH FLOWER ~ Small curved lines of chain stitch finished with a short straight stitch on the end. As this line of stitching is so fine, a stabbing motion is recommended.

 FRENCH KNOT FLOWERS ~ All french knots have a single twist unless otherwise stated.

 GRUB ~ Body – a long bullion of about twelve wraps; head – a french knot of two or three twists; antennae – two short straight stitches in a 'V' shape on top of the head.

No. 963: 2 strands

�֎	daisy
✤	forget-me-not
ₒ°	french knots 2 twists
⊥⊻	small star
⚘	long-tack daisy
✻	aster
▪	straight stitch
↯	fuchsia
°	french knot

No. 524: 1 strand

⌣	couched stem or tendril
↑	straight stitch
0	leaf
•	french knot

16

No. 3727: 2 strands

𝟢   small rosebud

𝑜   french knot
2 twists

𝑜   french knot

❟   straight stitch

✻   daisy

No. 818: 2 strands

𝟢   small rosebud

●   french knot
2 twists

✤   daisy

No. 3727: 1 strand

3 small daisies at the top of the letter

3 small buttons (5mm/ ¼" diameter)

Mill Hill Petite glass beads No. 40123

No. 524: 1 strand

\ ⌒   couched stem or tendril

◊   leaf

Ʋ   fly stitch

∧ ᵛ   straight stitch

.   french knot

18

No. 745: 2 strands

⌀	small rosebud
o	french knot
⚘	daisy
⚘	daisy bud

No. 524: 1 strand

) ⌒	couched stem or tendril
◊	leaf
⅄	straight stitch
•	french knot
⋎	fly stitch

Cupid charm
(see page 4)

No. 353: 1 strand

🌿	rosebud
🌸	rose
✳	bullion daisy
🌼	long-tack daisy

No. 353: 2 strands

☆ ☆	small stars
⦵	french knots
✱	aster
🍀	forget-me-not

No. 3743: 2 strands

⦵	french knots

No. 524: 1 strand

⌒ ⌒	couched stem or tendril
√ ↓	straight stitch
◖ ◗	leaf
⋅ ⋮	french knot

No. 524: 1 strand

) couched stem or tendril

ı⁄. straight stitch

◊ ⌀ leaf

⋰. french knots

No. 3354: 1 strand

  buttonhole flower

▽ bud

No. 3354: 2 strands

∞
○ french knots

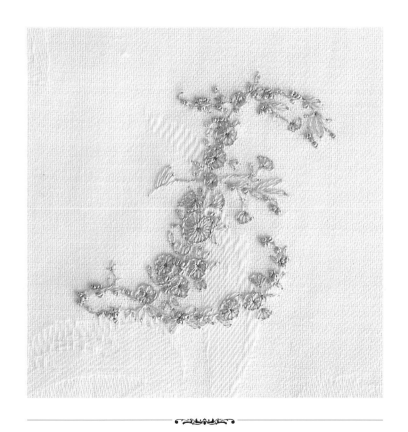

No. 745: 2 strands

✿ satin stitch flower

❀ large daisy

° °° french knots

No. 754: 2 strands

✴ satin stitch flower

° °° french knots

❀ forget-me-not

Note:

All satin stitch flowers are finished with a single strand french knot in the centre, using No. 3064 as the suggested colour. The large daisies have three or four single strand french knots to fill the centre. The same colour is used for the centres of the satin stitch flowers.

No. 524: 1 strand

∕⌒ couched stem or tendril

✔ leaf

No. 754: 1 strand

✴ buttonhole flower

No. 524: 1 strand

couched stem or tendril

leaf

fly stitch

No. 3608: 1 strand

small rosebud

No. 3608: 2 strands

french knots

No. 3609: 1 strand

rose

small rosebuds

No. 3609: 2 strands

french knots

✗   Mill Hill Petite glass beads No. 42024

Nos. 210, 211: 1 strand each combined

 french knots

No. 211: 2 strands

french knots

No. 761: 1 strand

small rosebuds

No. 761: 2 strands

french knots

No. 524: 1 strand

couched stem or tendril

leaf

fly stitch

No. 800: 2 strands

✿ daisy

✹ satin stitch flowers

❀ french knot

✿ daisy buds

❀ forget-me-not

No. 524: 1 strand

couched stem or tendril

leaf

cameo button

No. 605: 2 strands

⊛ buttonhole flower

〰 bud

ο french knots
ο ο

No. 605: 1 strand

🌹 rose

🥀 small rosebud

No. 524: 1 strand

⌣ ⌐ couched stem or tendril

◊◊ leaf

∨ ∨ fly stitch

No. 524: 1 strand

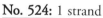 couched stem or tendril

leaf

No. 211: 1 strand

 lavender

No. 211: 2 strands

 daisy

 aster

 bud

 french knots

No. 754: 2 strands

鸞 rose

✳ daisy

°₀ french knots

✿ daisy bud

No. 754: 1 strand

𝌀 ₒ small rosebuds

chain stitch

No. 524: 1 strand

∫ ⌐ couched stem or tendril

◗ ◖ leaf

∨ ∨ fly stitch

Colour optional:

⬌ grub

38

Nos. 340, 341: 1 strand each combined

   satin stitch flower

🏵️   forget-me-not

∞ᵒ   french knots

No. 524: 1 strand

◠⁄   couched stem or tendril

◗◗   leaf

No. 963: 2 strands

🏵️   forget-me-not

ᵒ∞ₒ   french knots

40

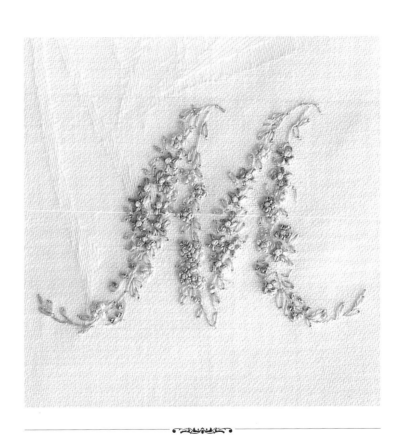

41

No. 745: 1 strand

🌀 rose

𝖀 rosebud

𝌀 small rosebud

No. 745: 2 strands

°°°° french knots
°

✗ Mill Hill Petite glass
beads No. 40557

No. 524: 1 strand

⌒ couched stem or tendril

◊ leaf

√ ∨ fly stitch

No. 524: 1 strand

couched stem or tendril

leaf

fly stitch

No. 3608: 2 strands

large daisy

french knots

No. 3609: 2 strands

rose

small rosebud

daisy

small stars

No. 3609: 1 strand

small rosebuds

44

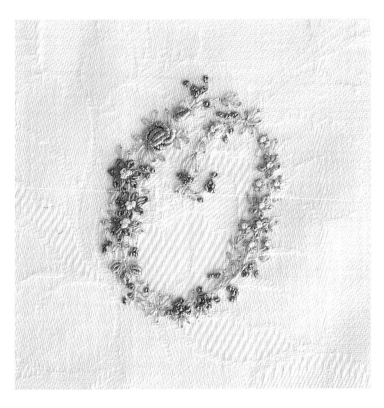

No. 524: 1 strand

- couched stem or tendril
- leaf
- straight stitch
- fly stitch

No. 754: 1 strand

- small rosebuds

No. 754: 2 strands

- rose
- small star
- aster
- daisy
- fuchsia
- french knots

No. 605: 1 strand

⊘   small rosebud

No. 605: 2 strands

✳   large daisy

✳   daisy

⦚   straight stitches

⅋   fuchsias

∞   french knots

No. 524: 1 strand

⌒   couched stem or tendril

ℳ   leaf

Y   fly stitch

A.Smith

No. 341: 1 strand

𝒐 small rosebuds
𝒐

No. 524: 1 strand

⟨ couched stem or tendril

◊◊ leaf

∨ ∨ fly stitch

No. 341: 2 strands

✻ daisy

❀ forget-me-not

°
∞ french knots

No. 605: 1 strand

small rosebuds

chain stitch

buttonhole buds

No. 524: 1 strand

couched stem or tendril

leaf

fly stitch

No. 605: 2 strands

satin stitch flowers

french knots

No. 3747: 1 strand

small rosebuds

No. 818: 2 strands

large daisy (surrounding button)

french knots

satin stitch flower

No. 818: 1 strand

small rosebuds

Optional:

small 5mm/¼" button

Secure the button in position with a bullion stitch worked through the holes.

Mill Hill Petite glass beads No. 40123

No. 524: 1 strand

couched stem or tendril

leaf

fly stitch

No. 3747: 2 strands

satin stitch flowers

french knots

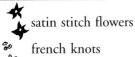

54

No. 3609: 1 strand

🌹 rose

𝟶 𝟶 small rosebuds

◭ ◮ buttonhole bud

.·˙ french knots

No. 524: 1 strand

⌒ couched stem or tendril

◖ leaf

∨ ⋁ fly stitch

No. 3609: 2 strands

✿ daisy

🌸 🌸 forget-me-nots

˚° french knots
°°°

No. 754: 1 strand

chain stitch

long-tack daisy

small rosebuds

No. 754: 2 strands

french knots

No. 745: 1 strand

small rosebuds

No. 745: 2 strands

french knots

No. 524: 1 strand

couched stem or tendril

leaf

fly stitch

No. 353: 2 strands

daisy

daisy buds

forget-me-nots

french knots

long-tack daisy

No. 524: 1 strand

couched stem or tendril

leaf

fly stitch

No. 353: 1 strand

small rosebuds

grub – 1 strand in colour of your choice (or No. 731 optional)

60

No. 524: 1 strand

couched stem or tendril

leaf

fly stitch

No. 818: 1 strand

small rosebuds

long-tack daisy

No. 341: 2 strands

satin stitch flowers

forget-me-nots

french knots

No. 818: 2 strands

french knots

small star

No. 524: 1 strand

couched stem or tendril

leaf

fly stitch

No. 745: 2 strands

satin stitch flower

french knots

No. 745: 1 strand

buttonhole flower

small rosebuds

Note:

Centres of satin stitch flowers and buttonhole flowers finished with french knot in 2 strands of No. 407.

No. 605: 2 strands

rose

daisy

french knots

No. 524: 1 strand

couched stem or tendril

leaf

fly stitch

No. 605: 1 strand

small rosebuds